World Builder

a step-by-step workbook to
Building Rich Worlds

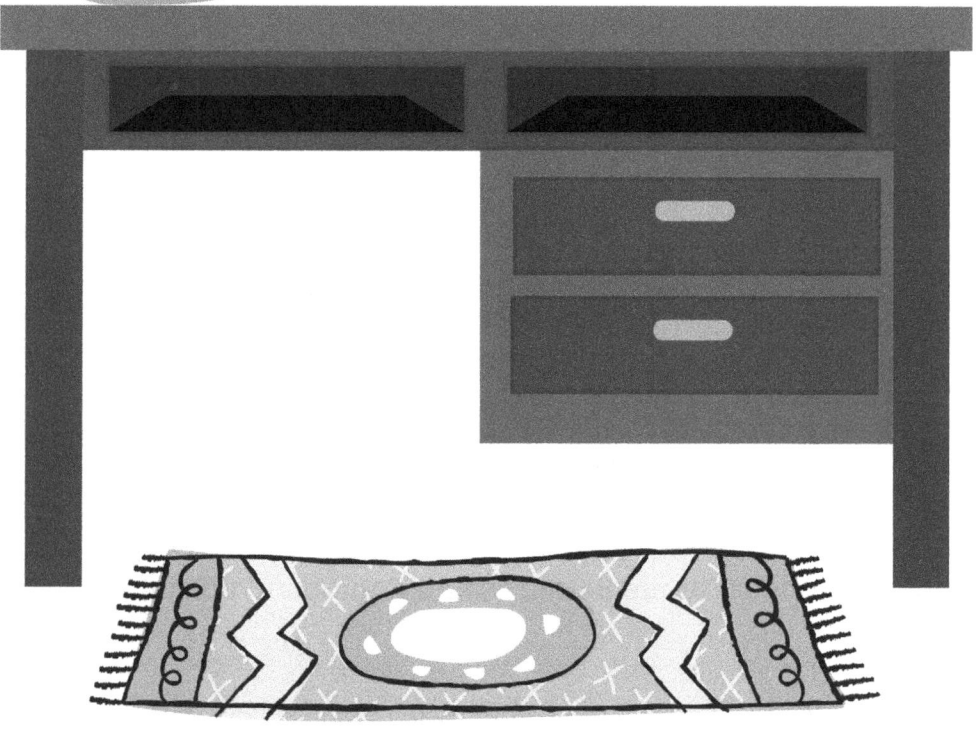

Author by Design

Caption

World Builder Copyright © 2021

World Builder is an excerpt from the Book and Series Builders (formerly the Book and Series Bibles).

Author By Design, Connie Bauldree and BaulConn Publishing Group.

All rights reserved. No part of this publication may be reproduced, stored in a retrieval system, or transmitted in any form or by any means electronic, mechanical, photocopying, recording, or otherwise without prior written permission of the publisher and copyright owner.

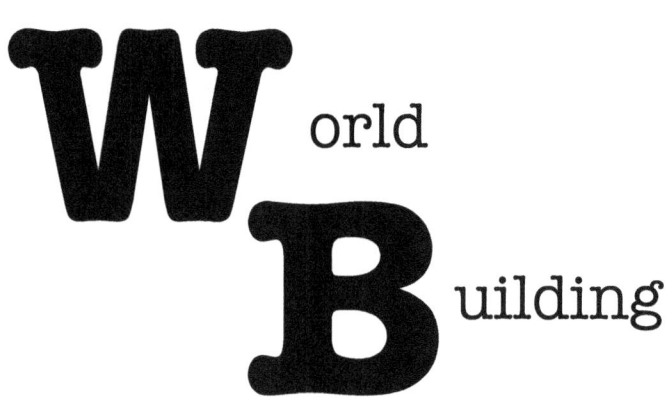

World Building

Building a world can be fun but also, daunting. There are so many elements that go into world building. The following pages are full of questions to help guide you in this process. I hope they spark more questions so that you can create the best world possible for your book!

World Name

Universe

Est. Population

World Building Questions

Write a brief description of your world (1-2 sentences).

_____

_____

_____

_____

When was your world created?

_____

How was your world created?

_____

_____

What are the laws of physics in your world?

_____

_____

_____

How does your world's solar system work?

_____

_____

_____

What is your world's plant life like? Are there any plants that are magical? Poisonous?

_____

_____

_____

Are there different plants in different regions of your world? Describe.

_____

_____

_____

_____

Are there mountains, forests, rivers, deserts, seas, oceans, etc. in your world?

_____

_____

_____

_____

What type of animals and/or creatures inhabit your world?

_____

_____

_____

_____

How did these animals/creatures evolve?

_____

_____

_____

_____

Are there different animals/creatures in different regions? Describe.

_____

_____

_____

_____

What types of insects inhabit your world?

_____

_____

_____

_____

Are there different insects in different regions? Describe.

_____

_____

_____

_____

What is the capital city of your world? Describe this city's importance.

_____

_____

_____

_____

What are the names of the other major cities in your world? Which ones are most populated?

_____

_____

_____

_____

Do your cities each have their own identity (laws, crests, flags, colors, etc.)? If so, describe.

_____

_____

_____

_____

What is the climate like in your world?

_____

_____

_____

_____

Does the climate differ in each region? If so, how?

_____

_____

_____

_____

Are there seasons in your world? How many and what are they called?

_____

_____

_____

_____

Is there anything out of the ordinary about your climate or anything that can manipulate your climate?

_____

_____

_____

_____

What type of species or races populate your world?

_____

_____

_____

_____

How did these species/races come into existence?

_____

_____

_____

_____

Is there any segregation or discrimination that occurs amongst your species/races?
Describe.

_____

_____

_____

_____

What, if any, distinguishing features do each of your species/races exhibit? Do any features
make it easy to identify the different kinds?

_____

_____

_____

_____

How are the people in your world governed?

_____

_____

_____

_____

What customs or rituals are practiced in your world?

_____

_____

_____

_____

What types of celebrations or traditions are practiced in your world? Weddings, funerals, festivals, etc.

_____

_____

_____

_____

What languages are spoken in your world? Does each region have its own language?

_____

_____

_____

_____

Is there a universal language? If so, which one?

_____

_____

_____

_____

Is there an economic and/or social class system? If so, describe it.

_____

_____

_____

_____

How are family units structured? (i.e. mom, dad, patriarchal, matriarchal, etc.)?

_____

_____

_____

_____

Does marriage exist in your world? If so, how is it defined?

_____

_____

_____

_____

Describe the history of your world. When did you civilization begin? Where there any significant wars? Is there any reason why your regions were created that can be traced back to turmoil or significant events? The sky's the limit, detail your history as little or as much as you'd like.

_____

_____

_____

_____

_____

_____

_____

_____

_____

_____

_____

_____

_____

_____

_____

_____

_____

Does religion exist in your world? If so, what is the religion? Are there many different type? Does it vary by region? Species?

_____

_____

_____

_____

Are there Gods and/or deities in your world? Describe.

_____

_____

_____

_____

Are there any significant prophets in your world? Region Specific? Describe.

_____

_____

_____

_____

Define the different cultures within your world.

_____

_____

_____

_____

Describe literature, art and music. Is each region different?

_____

_____

_____

_____

_____

Describe the clothing. Is each region different? What is the difference between men, women, species and race?

_____

_____

_____

_____

What type of cuisine is in your world? Is there a difference between regions, species or economic/social class?

_____

_____

_____

Does formal education exist in your world? If so, what does this system look like? Is it available to everyone?

_____

_____

_____

_____

What types of things are available for leisure in your world? Do different species have different actives? Do economic and social class affect this?

_____

_____

_____

_____

What is the most common type of leisure activity?

_____

_____

_____

_____

What is the economy like in your world? Does it vary by region, by class or by species?

_____

_____

_____

_____

What cities/regions are allies in trade? Has this changed over time?

_____

_____

_____

_____

Is there a common currency throughout the world? If not, what different types of currency are used?

_____

_____

_____

_____

Describe natural resources throughout the world. How are they traded? Which regions benefit from them the most? How do they affect relationships?

_____

_____

_____

_____

What types of transportation are available in your world?

_____

_____

_____

_____

What businesses are profitable? Are certain businesses considered more elite than others?
How are they structured?

_____

_____

_____

_____

What is a normal work schedule? Average pay rate?

_____

_____

_____

_____

Are there organized crime groups within businesses?

_____

_____

_____

_____

How easy is it to start a new business in your world?

_____

_____

_____

_____

If magic is prevalent in your world, what are the rules of that magic?

_____

_____

_____

_____

Is there a hierarchy of magicians? If so, how is that structured?

_____

_____

_____

_____

Who can use magic? Is it species specific? Social or economical class specific?

_____

_____

_____

_____

How does society feel about magic in your world? Is it regulated in any way?

_____

_____

_____

_____

Describe the government in your world. Is it a monarchy, republic, empire, democracy, theocracy, etc.?

_____

_____

_____

_____

What is the justice system in your world? How does it function? Are there laws, punishments, etc.?

_____

_____

_____

_____

Is there a military in your world? If so, describe.

_____

_____

_____

_____

Does your world have advanced technology? If so, describe.

_____

_____

_____

_____

Does your world have weapons? Are they predominant in certain areas?

_____

_____

_____

_____

Are there any special weapons? Who makes them and how do they work?

_____

_____

_____

_____

Are there weapons that any member of society can own? Weapons that are common amongst households?

_____

_____

_____

_____

World Building Notes

World Building Notes

Draw Your World

Draw Your World

Objects/Artifacts

Sketch	Description

Sketch	Description

Sketch	Description

Sketch	Description

Objects/Artifacts

Sketch	Description

Sketch	Description

Sketch	Description

Sketch	Description

World Name

Universe

Est. Population

World Building Questions

Write a brief description of your world (1-2 sentences).

_____

_____

_____

_____

When was your world created?

_____

How was your world created?

_____

_____

What are the laws of physics in your world?

_____

_____

_____

How does your world's solar system work?

_____

_____

_____

What is your world's plant life like? Are there any plants that are magical? Poisonous?

_____

_____

_____

Are there different plants in different regions of your world? Describe.

_____

_____

_____

_____

Are there mountains, forests, rivers, deserts, seas, oceans, etc. in your world?

_____

_____

_____

_____

What type of animals and/or creatures inhabit your world?

_____

_____

_____

_____

How did these animals/creatures evolve?

_____

_____

_____

_____

Are there different animals/creatures in different regions? Describe.

_____

_____

_____

_____

What types of insects inhabit your world?

_____

_____

_____

_____

Are there different insects in different regions? Describe.

_____

_____

_____

_____

What is the capital city of your world? Describe this city's importance.

_____

_____

_____

_____

What are the names of the other major cities in your world? Which ones are most populated?

_____

_____

_____

_____

Do your cities each have their own identity (laws, crests, flags, colors, etc.)? If so, describe.

_____

_____

_____

_____

What is the climate like in your world?

_____

_____

_____

_____

Does the climate differ in each region? If so, how?

_____

_____

_____

_____

Are there seasons in your world? How many and what are they called?

_____

_____

_____

_____

Is there anything out of the ordinary about your climate or anything that can manipulate your climate?

_____

_____

_____

_____

What type of species or races populate your world?

_____

_____

_____

_____

How did these species/races come into existence?

_____

_____

_____

_____

Is there any segregation or discrimination that occurs amongst your species/races?
Describe.

_____

_____

_____

_____

What, if any, distinguishing features do each of your species/races exhibit? Do any features
make it easy to identify the different kinds?

_____

_____

_____

_____

How are the people in your world governed?

_____

_____

_____

_____

What customs or rituals are practiced in your world?

_____

_____

_____

_____

What types of celebrations or traditions are practiced in your world? Weddings, funerals, festivals, etc.

_____

_____

_____

_____

What languages are spoken in your world? Does each region have its own language?

_____

_____

_____

_____

Is there a universal language? If so, which one?

_____

_____

_____

_____

Is there an economic and/or social class system? If so, describe it.

_____

_____

_____

_____

How are family units structured? (i.e. mom, dad, patriarchal, matriarchal, etc.)?

_____

_____

_____

_____

Does marriage exist in your world? If so, how is it defined?

_____

_____

_____

_____

Describe the history of your world. When did you civilization begin? Where there any significant wars? Is there any reason why your regions were created that can be traced back to turmoil or significant events? The sky's the limit, detail your history as little or as much as you'd like.

_____

_____

_____

_____

_____

_____

_____

_____

_____

_____

_____

_____

_____

_____

_____

_____

_____

Does religion exist in your world? If so, what is the religion? Are there many different type? Does it vary by region? Species?

_____

_____

_____

_____

Are there Gods and/or deities in your world? Describe.

_____

_____

_____

_____

Are there any significant prophets in your world? Region Specific? Describe.

_____

_____

_____

_____

Define the different cultures within your world.

_____

_____

_____

Describe literature, art and music. Is each region different?

_____

_____

_____

_____

_____

Describe the clothing. Is each region different? What is the difference between men, women, species and race?

_____

_____

_____

_____

What type of cuisine is in your world? Is there a difference between regions, species or economic/social class?

_____

_____

_____

Does formal education exist in your world? If so, what does this system look like? Is it available to everyone?

_____

_____

_____

_____

What types of things are available for leisure in your world? Do different species have different actives? Do economic and social class affect this?

_____

_____

_____

_____

What is the most common type of leisure activity?

_____

_____

_____

_____

What is the economy like in your world? Does it vary by region, by class or by species?

_____

_____

_____

_____

What cities/regions are allies in trade? Has this changed over time?

_____

_____

_____

_____

Is there a common currency throughout the world? If not, what different types of currency are used?

_____

_____

_____

_____

Describe natural resources throughout the world. How are they traded? Which regions benefit from them the most? How do they affect relationships?

_____

_____

_____

_____

What types of transportation are available in your world?

_____

_____

_____

_____

What businesses are profitable? Are certain businesses considered more elite than others? How are they structured?

_____

_____

_____

_____

What is a normal work schedule? Average pay rate?

_____

_____

_____

_____

Are there organized crime groups within businesses?

_____

_____

_____

_____

How easy is it to start a new business in your world?

_____

_____

_____

_____

If magic is prevalent in your world, what are the rules of that magic?

_____

_____

_____

_____

Is there a hierarchy of magicians? If so, how is that structured?

_____

_____

_____

_____

Who can use magic? Is it species specific? Social or economical class specific?

_____

_____

_____

_____

How does society feel about magic in your world? Is it regulated in any way?

_____

_____

_____

_____

Describe the government in your world. Is it a monarchy, republic, empire, democracy, theocracy, etc.?

_____

_____

_____

_____

What is the justice system in your world? How does it function? Are there laws, punishments, etc.?

_____

_____

_____

_____

Is there a military in your world? If so, describe.

_____

_____

_____

_____

Does your world have advanced technology? If so, describe.

_____

_____

_____

_____

Does your world have weapons? Are they predominant in certain areas?

_____

_____

_____

_____

Are there any special weapons? Who makes them and how do they work?

_____

_____

_____

_____

Are there weapons that any member of society can own? Weapons that are common amongst households?

_____

_____

_____

_____

World Building Notes

World Building Notes

Draw Your World

Draw Your World

Objects/Artifacts

Sketch	Description

Sketch	Description

Sketch	Description

Sketch	Description

Objects/Artifacts

Sketch	Description

Sketch	Description

Sketch	Description

Sketch	Description

World Name

Universe

Est. Population

World Building Questions

Write a brief description of your world (1-2 sentences).

_____

_____

_____

When was your world created?

_____

How was your world created?

_____

_____

What are the laws of physics in your world?

_____

_____

_____

How does your world's solar system work?

_____

_____

_____

What is your world's plant life like? Are there any plants that are magical? Poisonous?

_____

_____

_____

Are there different plants in different regions of your world? Describe.

_____

_____

_____

_____

Are there mountains, forests, rivers, deserts, seas, oceans, etc. in your world?

_____

_____

_____

_____

What type of animals and/or creatures inhabit your world?

_____

_____

_____

_____

How did these animals/creatures evolve?

_____

_____

_____

_____

Are there different animals/creatures in different regions? Describe.

_____

_____

_____

_____

What types of insects inhabit your world?

_____

_____

_____

_____

Are there different insects in different regions? Describe.

_____

_____

_____

_____

What is the capital city of your world? Describe this city's importance.

_____

_____

_____

_____

What are the names of the other major cities in your world? Which ones are most populated?

_____

_____

_____

_____

Do your cities each have their own identity (laws, crests, flags, colors, etc.)? If so, describe.

_____

_____

_____

_____

What is the climate like in your world?

_____

_____

_____

_____

Does the climate differ in each region? If so, how?

_____

_____

_____

_____

Are there seasons in your world? How many and what are they called?

_____

_____

_____

_____

Is there anything out of the ordinary about your climate or anything that can manipulate your climate?

_____

_____

_____

_____

What type of species or races populate your world?

_____

_____

_____

_____

How did these species/races come into existence?

_____

_____

_____

_____

Is there any segregation or discrimination that occurs amongst your species/races?
Describe.

_____

_____

_____

_____

What, if any, distinguishing features do each of your species/races exhibit? Do any features
make it easy to identify the different kinds?

_____

_____

_____

_____

How are the people in your world governed?

_____

_____

_____

_____

What customs or rituals are practiced in your world?

_____

_____

_____

_____

What types of celebrations or traditions are practiced in your world? Weddings, funerals, festivals, etc.

_____

_____

_____

_____

What languages are spoken in your world? Does each region have its own language?

_____

_____

_____

_____

Is there a universal language? If so, which one?

_____

_____

_____

_____

Is there an economic and/or social class system? If so, describe it.

_____

_____

_____

_____

How are family units structured? (i.e. mom, dad, patriarchal, matriarchal, etc.)?

_____

_____

_____

_____

Does marriage exist in your world? If so, how is it defined?

_____

_____

_____

_____

Describe the history of your world. When did you civilization begin? Where there any significant wars? Is there any reason why your regions were created that can be traced back to turmoil or significant events? The sky's the limit, detail your history as little or as much as you'd like.

_____

_____

_____

_____

_____

_____

_____

_____

_____

_____

_____

_____

_____

_____

_____

_____

_____

Does religion exist in your world? If so, what is the religion? Are there many different type? Does it vary by region? Species?

_____

_____

_____

_____

Are there Gods and/or deities in your world? Describe.

_____

_____

_____

_____

Are there any significant prophets in your world? Region Specific? Describe.

_____

_____

_____

_____

Define the different cultures within your world.

_____

_____

_____

Describe literature, art and music. Is each region different?

_____

_____

_____

_____

Describe the clothing. Is each region different? What is the difference between men, women, species and race?

_____

_____

_____

_____

What type of cuisine is in your world? Is there a difference between regions, species or economic/social class?

_____

_____

_____

_____

Does formal education exist in your world? If so, what does this system look like? Is it available to everyone?

_____

_____

_____

_____

What types of things are available for leisure in your world? Do different species have different actives? Do economic and social class affect this?

_____

_____

_____

_____

What is the most common type of leisure activity?

_____

_____

_____

_____

What is the economy like in your world? Does it vary by region, by class or by species?

_____

_____

_____

_____

What cities/regions are allies in trade? Has this changed over time?

_____

_____

_____

_____

Is there a common currency throughout the world? If not, what different types of currency are used?

_____

_____

_____

_____

Describe natural resources throughout the world. How are they traded? Which regions benefit from them the most? How do they affect relationships?

_____

_____

_____

_____

What types of transportation are available in your world?

_____

_____

_____

_____

What businesses are profitable? Are certain businesses considered more elite than others? How are they structured?

_____

_____

_____

_____

What is a normal work schedule? Average pay rate?

_____

_____

_____

_____

Are there organized crime groups within businesses?

_____

_____

_____

_____

How easy is it to start a new business in your world?

_____

_____

_____

_____

If magic is prevalent in your world, what are the rules of that magic?

_____

_____

_____

_____

Is there a hierarchy of magicians? If so, how is that structured?

_____

_____

_____

_____

Who can use magic? Is it species specific? Social or economical class specific?

_____

_____

_____

_____

How does society feel about magic in your world? Is it regulated in any way?

_____

_____

_____

_____

Describe the government in your world. Is it a monarchy, republic, empire, democracy, theocracy, etc.?

_____

_____

_____

_____

What is the justice system in your world? How does it function? Are there laws, punishments, etc.?

_____

_____

_____

_____

Is there a military in your world? If so, describe.

_____

_____

_____

_____

Does your world have advanced technology? If so, describe.

_____

_____

_____

_____

Does your world have weapons? Are they predominant in certain areas?

_____

_____

_____

_____

Are there any special weapons? Who makes them and how do they work?

_____

_____

_____

_____

Are there weapons that any member of society can own? Weapons that are common amongst households?

_____

_____

_____

_____

_____

World Building Notes

World Building Notes

Draw Your World

Draw Your World

Objects/Artifacts

Sketch	Description

Sketch	Description

Sketch	Description

Sketch	Description

Objects/Artifacts

Sketch	Description

Sketch	Description

Sketch	Description

Sketch	Description

World Name

Universe

Est. Population

World Building Questions

Write a brief description of your world (1-2 sentences).

_____

_____

_____

_____

When was your world created?

_____

How was your world created?

_____

_____

What are the laws of physics in your world?

_____

_____

_____

How does your world's solar system work?

_____

_____

_____

What is your world's plant life like? Are there any plants that are magical? Poisonous?

_____

_____

_____

Are there different plants in different regions of your world? Describe.

_____

_____

_____

_____

Are there mountains, forests, rivers, deserts, seas, oceans, etc. in your world?

_____

_____

_____

_____

What type of animals and/or creatures inhabit your world?

_____

_____

_____

_____

How did these animals/creatures evolve?

_____

_____

_____

_____

Are there different animals/creatures in different regions? Describe.

_____

_____

_____

_____

What types of insects inhabit your world?

_____

_____

_____

_____

Are there different insects in different regions? Describe.

_____

_____

_____

_____

What is the capital city of your world? Describe this city's importance.

_____

_____

_____

_____

What are the names of the other major cities in your world? Which ones are most populated?

_____

_____

_____

_____

Do your cities each have their own identity (laws, crests, flags, colors, etc.)? If so, describe.

_____

_____

_____

_____

What is the climate like in your world?

_____

_____

_____

_____

Does the climate differ in each region? If so, how?

_____

_____

_____

_____

Are there seasons in your world? How many and what are they called?

_____

_____

_____

_____

Is there anything out of the ordinary about your climate or anything that can manipulate your climate?

_____

_____

_____

_____

What type of species or races populate your world?

_____

_____

_____

_____

How did these species/races come into existence?

_____

_____

_____

_____

Is there any segregation or discrimination that occurs amongst your species/races? Describe.

_____

_____

_____

_____

What, if any, distinguishing features do each of your species/races exhibit? Do any features make it easy to identify the different kinds?

_____

_____

_____

_____

How are the people in your world governed?

_____

_____

_____

_____

What customs or rituals are practiced in your world?

_____

_____

_____

_____

What types of celebrations or traditions are practiced in your world? Weddings, funerals, festivals, etc.

_____

_____

_____

_____

What languages are spoken in your world? Does each region have its own language?

_____

_____

_____

_____

Is there a universal language? If so, which one?

_____

_____

_____

_____

Is there an economic and/or social class system? If so, describe it.

_____

_____

_____

_____

How are family units structured? (i.e. mom, dad, patriarchal, matriarchal, etc.)?

_____

_____

_____

_____

Does marriage exist in your world? If so, how is it defined?

_____

_____

_____

_____

Describe the history of your world. When did you civilization begin? Where there any significant wars? Is there any reason why your regions were created that can be traced back to turmoil or significant events? The sky's the limit, detail your history as little or as much as you'd like.

_____

_____

_____

_____

_____

_____

_____

_____

_____

_____

_____

_____

_____

_____

_____

_____

_____

_____

Does religion exist in your world? If so, what is the religion? Are there many different type? Does it vary by region? Species?

_____

_____

_____

_____

Are there Gods and/or deities in your world? Describe.

_____

_____

_____

_____

Are there any significant prophets in your world? Region Specific? Describe.

_____

_____

_____

_____

Define the different cultures within your world.

_____

_____

_____

_____

Describe literature, art and music. Is each region different?

_____

_____

_____

_____

Describe the clothing. Is each region different? What is the difference between men, women, species and race?

_____

_____

_____

_____

What type of cuisine is in your world? Is there a difference between regions, species or economic/social class?

_____

_____

_____

_____

Does formal education exist in your world? If so, what does this system look like? Is it available to everyone?

_____

_____

_____

_____

What types of things are available for leisure in your world? Do different species have different actives? Do economic and social class affect this?

_____

_____

_____

_____

What is the most common type of leisure activity?

_____

_____

_____

_____

What is the economy like in your world? Does it vary by region, by class or by species?

_____

_____

_____

_____

What cities/regions are allies in trade? Has this changed over time?

_____

_____

_____

_____

Is there a common currency throughout the world? If not, what different types of currency are used?

_____

_____

_____

_____

Describe natural resources throughout the world. How are they traded? Which regions benefit from them the most? How do they affect relationships?

_____

_____

_____

_____

What types of transportation are available in your world?

_____

_____

_____

_____

What businesses are profitable? Are certain businesses considered more elite than others? How are they structured?

_____

_____

_____

_____

What is a normal work schedule? Average pay rate?

_____

_____

_____

_____

Are there organized crime groups within businesses?

_____

_____

_____

_____

How easy is it to start a new business in your world?

_____

_____

_____

_____

If magic is prevalent in your world, what are the rules of that magic?

_____

_____

_____

_____

Is there a hierarchy of magicians? If so, how is that structured?

_____

_____

_____

_____

Who can use magic? Is it species specific? Social or economical class specific?

_____

_____

_____

_____

How does society feel about magic in your world? Is it regulated in any way?

_____

_____

_____

_____

Describe the government in your world. Is it a monarchy, republic, empire, democracy, theocracy, etc.?

_____

_____

_____

_____

What is the justice system in your world? How does it function? Are there laws, punishments, etc.?

_____

_____

_____

_____

Is there a military in your world? If so, describe.

_____

_____

_____

_____

Does your world have advanced technology? If so, describe.

_____

_____

_____

_____

Does your world have weapons? Are they predominant in certain areas?

_____

_____

_____

_____

Are there any special weapons? Who makes them and how do they work?

_____

_____

_____

_____

Are there weapons that any member of society can own? Weapons that are common amongst households?

_____

_____

_____

_____

World Building Notes

World Building Notes

Draw Your World

Draw Your World

Objects/Artifacts

Sketch	Description

Sketch	Description

Sketch	Description

Sketch	Description

Objects/Artifacts

Sketch	Description

Sketch	Description

Sketch	Description

Sketch	Description

World Name

Universe

Est. Population

World Building Questions

Write a brief description of your world (1-2 sentences).

_____

_____

_____

_____

When was your world created?

_____

How was your world created?

_____

_____

What are the laws of physics in your world?

_____

_____

_____

How does your world's solar system work?

_____

_____

_____

What is your world's plant life like? Are there any plants that are magical? Poisonous?

_____

_____

_____

Are there different plants in different regions of your world? Describe.

_____

_____

_____

_____

Are there mountains, forests, rivers, deserts, seas, oceans, etc. in your world?

_____

_____

_____

_____

What type of animals and/or creatures inhabit your world?

_____

_____

_____

_____

How did these animals/creatures evolve?

_____

_____

_____

_____

Are there different animals/creatures in different regions? Describe.

_____

_____

_____

_____

What types of insects inhabit your world?

_____

_____

_____

_____

Are there different insects in different regions? Describe.

_____

_____

_____

_____

What is the capital city of your world? Describe this city's importance.

_____

_____

_____

_____

What are the names of the other major cities in your world? Which ones are most populated?

_____

_____

_____

_____

Do your cities each have their own identity (laws, crests, flags, colors, etc.)? If so, describe.

_____

_____

_____

_____

What is the climate like in your world?

_____

_____

_____

_____

Does the climate differ in each region? If so, how?

_____

_____

_____

_____

Are there seasons in your world? How many and what are they called?

_____

_____

_____

_____

Is there anything out of the ordinary about your climate or anything that can manipulate your climate?

_____

_____

_____

_____

What type of species or races populate your world?

_____

_____

_____

_____

How did these species/races come into existence?

_____

_____

_____

_____

Is there any segregation or discrimination that occurs amongst your species/races? Describe.

_____

_____

_____

_____

What, if any, distinguishing features do each of your species/races exhibit? Do any features make it easy to identify the different kinds?

_____

_____

_____

_____

How are the people in your world governed?

_____

_____

_____

_____

What customs or rituals are practiced in your world?

_____

_____

_____

_____

What types of celebrations or traditions are practiced in your world? Weddings, funerals, festivals, etc.

_____

_____

_____

_____

What languages are spoken in your world? Does each region have its own language?

_____

_____

_____

_____

Is there a universal language? If so, which one?

_____

_____

_____

_____

Is there an economic and/or social class system? If so, describe it.

_____

_____

_____

_____

How are family units structured? (i.e. mom, dad, patriarchal, matriarchal, etc.)?

_____

_____

_____

_____

Does marriage exist in your world? If so, how is it defined?

_____

_____

_____

_____

Describe the history of your world. When did you civilization begin? Where there any significant wars? Is there any reason why your regions were created that can be traced back to turmoil or significant events? The sky's the limit, detail your history as little or as much as you'd like.

_____

_____

_____

_____

_____

_____

_____

_____

_____

_____

_____

_____

_____

_____

_____

_____

_____

_____

Does religion exist in your world? If so, what is the religion? Are there many different type? Does it vary by region? Species?

_____

_____

_____

_____

Are there Gods and/or deities in your world? Describe.

_____

_____

_____

_____

Are there any significant prophets in your world? Region Specific? Describe.

_____

_____

_____

_____

Define the different cultures within your world.

_____

_____

_____

_____

Describe literature, art and music. Is each region different?

_____

_____

_____

_____

Describe the clothing. Is each region different? What is the difference between men, women, species and race?

_____

_____

_____

_____

What type of cuisine is in your world? Is there a difference between regions, species or economic/social class?

_____

_____

_____

_____

Does formal education exist in your world? If so, what does this system look like? Is it available to everyone?

_____

_____

_____

_____

What types of things are available for leisure in your world? Do different species have different actives? Do economic and social class affect this?

_____

_____

_____

_____

What is the most common type of leisure activity?

_____

_____

_____

_____

What is the economy like in your world? Does it vary by region, by class or by species?

_____

_____

_____

_____

What cities/regions are allies in trade? Has this changed over time?

_____

_____

_____

_____

Is there a common currency throughout the world? If not, what different types of currency are used?

_____

_____

_____

_____

Describe natural resources throughout the world. How are they traded? Which regions benefit from them the most? How do they affect relationships?

_____

_____

_____

_____

What types of transportation are available in your world?

_____

_____

_____

_____

What businesses are profitable? Are certain businesses considered more elite than others? How are they structured?

_____

_____

_____

_____

What is a normal work schedule? Average pay rate?

_____

_____

_____

_____

Are there organized crime groups within businesses?

_____

_____

_____

_____

How easy is it to start a new business in your world?

_____

_____

_____

_____

If magic is prevalent in your world, what are the rules of that magic?

_____

_____

_____

_____

Is there a hierarchy of magicians? If so, how is that structured?

_____

_____

_____

_____

Who can use magic? Is it species specific? Social or economical class specific?

_____

_____

_____

_____

How does society feel about magic in your world? Is it regulated in any way?

_____

_____

_____

_____

Describe the government in your world. Is it a monarchy, republic, empire, democracy, theocracy, etc.?

_____

_____

_____

_____

What is the justice system in your world? How does it function? Are there laws, punishments, etc.?

_____

_____

_____

_____

Is there a military in your world? If so, describe.

_____

_____

_____

_____

Does your world have advanced technology? If so, describe.

_____

_____

_____

_____

Does your world have weapons? Are they predominant in certain areas?

_____

_____

_____

_____

Are there any special weapons? Who makes them and how do they work?

_____

_____

_____

_____

Are there weapons that any member of society can own? Weapons that are common amongst households?

_____

_____

_____

_____

World Building Notes

World Building Notes

Draw Your World

Draw Your World

Objects/Artifacts

Sketch	Description

Sketch	Description

Sketch	Description

Sketch	Description

Objects/Artifacts

Sketch	Description

Sketch	Description

Sketch	Description

Sketch	Description

Sketches **&** **N**otes

About the Author

Connie Bauldree, creator of Author by Design, lives in the Rocky Mountains with her loving husband and kids. She writes under several pen names and in several different genres. When she's not writing, she can be found playing taxi to teenagers and binge watching supernatural shows. Visit her at www.authorbydesign.co, follow her on FB @authorbydesign21 or email her at info@authorbydesign.co.

More Books & Fun...

Book Builder, Author by Design
This MUST HAVE book gives you one place to write your novel from start to finish. Available on Amazon.

Series Builder, Author by Design
This MUST HAVE book gives you one place to write your series from start to finish. Offering everything from the Book Builder and more. Available on Amazon.

Character Builder, Author by Design
An excerpt from the Book and Series Builders's. Create up to 50 characters in this stand alone Character Builder. Available on Amazon.

66 Day Author Planner, Author by Design
Want to build better writing habits? Then the 66 Day Author Challenge/Planner is for you! Coming soon!

Writer's Block Box, Author by Design
The only subscription box you'll ever need as an author! Fighting writer's block ... one author a time. www.writersblockboxes.com

www.ingramcontent.com/pod-product-compliance
Lightning Source LLC
Chambersburg PA
CBHW081506040426
42446CB00017B/3420